When the Mirror Talks Back

Dr. Sheree Johnson

First Edition

THE Hopeful NEST
Columbia, Maryland

Acknowledgements

Writing this book has been an amazing experience for me. Being able to turn my experiences and journey into a guide that helps others navigate their own process has brought me immense fulfillment. However, I couldn't have done it alone.

To my colleagues, loved ones, and my fiancé, Casey: Thank you for being my mirrors and my anchors. You've stood by me during my most challenging times without judgment, all while celebrating my growth. You've encouraged and inspired me to share my expertise, and for that, I am truly grateful to every one of you.

To my clients and readers: Thank you for inspiring this work and motivating me to keep going. You give my work purpose every day through your courage to heal, ask questions, and do the inner work. I will forever appreciate you for allowing me to be a part of your journey.

To every person who told me the truth, even when I didn't want to hear it, I thank you. You planted seeds in me that I didn't know I needed.

And finally, to my God: Thank you for your grace, strength, and the ability to finish what I've started.

Deep Regards,
Dr. Sheree Johnson

Contents

Introduction

———— ··•●•··

Have you ever found yourself stuck repeating the same issues with different names, faces, and settings? Never understanding why your relationships are so toxic? Wondering why happiness and peace seem so out of reach, while trying to figure out why things never change? It's easy to point fingers and blame others for your mishaps. But the truth is, it's not them. It's you. It's time to start looking within and identifying where change needs to begin.

When the Mirror Talks Back is not about feeling guilty or being ashamed of yourself. It's about understanding that the most important relationship you have is the one you build with yourself. It's about challenging yourself to look inward at your habits, your mindset, and your emotional patterns with honesty and compassion.

The mirror metaphor isn't just poetic. It's practical. When the mirror talks back, it shows you the patterns you've been blind to and reveals the unconscious choices that keep you stuck.

When the Mirror Talks Back invites you to pause, reflect, and go deeper through practical strategies and guided questions designed to spark self-awareness and personal growth. You'll learn tools for breaking unhealthy cycles, taking accountability, and embracing change to help you become a healthier and healed version of yourself.

Your growth and healing journey is about you, not them. The work isn't quick or easy. Real change takes courage and consistency. Start pouring into yourself by taking the time to read, understand, and apply the topics discussed in this book to your everyday life.

Let your transformation begin!

PART 1

The Awakening

Awareness & Accountability

Accountability

Accountability is the ability to look within yourself and acknowledge your actions or inactions without blaming others. It's the power to own your mistakes and wrongdoings. This means recognizing the role you played in a situation without adopting a victim mentality. You may find accountability difficult because you don't want to be held responsible for your actions. It's hard because it requires you to confront your flaws. It also demands self-reflection, humility, and the ability to say, "I was wrong." And that's not easy.

When you dodge accountability, you place the blame on others, circumstances, or anything but yourself. However, refusing to take responsibility only keeps you stuck, causing the same destructive patterns. Often, people avoid accountability because they fail to examine situations honestly. By overlooking your role in conflicts and failures, and choosing to be in denial, you only rob yourself of the opportunity to grow. Be brave enough to own your decisions, learn from your mistakes, and work toward becoming a better version of yourself. Embracing accountability is the first step toward self-improvement.

Struggling with taking ownership of your actions? Try this:

1. Be honest with yourself about your actions and your intentions.

2. Stop justifying poor behavior.

3. Resist the urge to blame others and own your choices. Learn to admit your faults.

4. Surround yourself with people who will hold you accountable.

Accountability

Am I focusing on finding excuses or finding solutions?

What role did I play in a recent situation where things didn't go as planned?

What could I have done differently? (Avoid blaming others)

How can avoiding accountability affect your relationships and reputation?

Self-Reflection

One of the most effective tools for understanding yourself and the world around you is self-reflection. It is the process of intentionally examining your thoughts, behaviors, and experiences with honest curiosity to understand the deeper patterns that drive your actions and relationships. Self-reflection is the tool that makes your mirror talk back; it's how you see yourself clearly instead of through the distorted lens of defensiveness, blame, or denial. This process helps you become self-aware and more in tune with yourself. The insight you gain from practicing self-reflection will help you better understand your thoughts, feelings, and behaviors. It also helps you identify your motivations, triggers, and habits.

Once you become skilled at self-reflection, you will notice improved decision-making, as your choices become more intentional and logical than emotional. Self-reflection requires accountability and helps you learn from your mistakes rather than repeating them. You can't fix what you don't acknowledge, and that's why it's important to be honest with yourself. Self-reflection isn't always comfortable; it requires courage to face truths about yourself that you might prefer to ignore. But this discomfort signals growth. If you want to improve your life and be more internally connected, self-reflection is non-negotiable.

Strategies for self-reflection:

1. Create space for solitude with no distractions.
2. Examine yourself and be honest about what's happening internally—what are you thinking and how are you feeling? Why are you thinking and feeling this way?

3. Check in with yourself—reflect on what happened, recognize what you learned, and reset by deciding what you want to do differently.

4. Make reflection a routine—develop the habit of regularly checking in with yourself.

Self-Reflection

What version of myself have I been showing up as lately?

In the past 30 days, what have I learned about myself emotionally, mentally, or spiritually?

What habits or mindsets have helped me grow personally or professionally? Which ones have hindered my growth?

Based on these reflections, what is one thing I want to change about how I show up moving forward?

Be a Person of Your Word

There is nothing more damaging to your relationships than being labeled as unreliable and flaky. We've all been on both sides of this: disappointed by others who don't follow through, and perhaps guilty of letting people down ourselves. That is why it is important to stand by your word. If you say you are going to do something, do it. Stand firm in your commitments and always strive to give 100 percent. Do not make promises you can't keep. Being a person of your word reflects accountability, integrity, and respect for others. When you are dependable and others can rely on you, that builds trust and nurtures healthy relationships.

When life happens and you are no longer able to fulfill a commitment, communicate that as soon as possible. Your words are just as vital as your actions; they should be honored and used wisely. Failing to be a person of your word can inconvenience others and negatively affect the way they view you. You damage your character when you don't stand by your word. Don't just talk about it. Be about it. Let your actions align with your words.

Strategies for helping you be a person of your word:

1. Avoid impulsive commitments—think carefully before you agree to anything.

2. Be realistic, stay within your limits, and don't exaggerate your abilities

3. Follow through on your commitments.

4. Consistently demonstrate reliability until it becomes second nature.

Be a Person of Your Word

Think of a time when you made a promise or commitment to yourself or someone else and didn't follow through. What happened?

What got in the way of you keeping your word?

How did not following through affect your relationship with that person or with yourself?

What would you do differently if faced with a similar situation today?

Check Your Attitude

Your attitude is one of your most valuable assets. How you treat others, how you respond to things, and how you show up for yourself and others says a lot about your character. Remember, your attitude will open doors that degrees and money can't. Treat others with respect and dignity regardless of their status. Your attitude is the energy you bring when you step into rooms, relationships, and opportunities. It's louder than your words and stronger than your resume. A negative attitude can be expensive. It could cost you relationships, opportunities, and the respect of others. Being authentic doesn't mean you have to be negative; you can be honest and still choose to approach situations constructively. Don't let a negative attitude rob you of your peace, purpose, or progress.

Having a positive attitude is more than being nice. It's about being guided by principles and being committed to doing what is right. A positive attitude doesn't mean pretending everything is fine. It means choosing to respond constructively even when things are difficult. A negative or positive attitude can be contagious, so be mindful of your approach. Cultivate the type of attitude that empowers, uplifts, and motivates others to do the same. Your attitude is what others see reflected back when they interact with you, so make sure it's a reflection that you're proud of.

How to check your attitude:

1. Practice self-awareness—pause and reflect on your attitude; be honest with yourself.

2. Monitor your reactions—how are you responding? Do you always need the last word? Are you defensive or dismissive? Or are you being gracious?

3. Examine your nonverbal communication; tone, body language, and overall energy.

4. Seek feedback from trusted people and remain open to criticism.

Check Your Attitude

How is my mood?

What situations or people tend to challenge my attitude the most, and what patterns do I notice in my responses?

What has my attitude been like lately, and how has this affected those around me?

If I could have the perfect attitude, how would I describe it? How can I make small changes daily to reflect it?

Stop Complaining

Imagine hearing the same boring tune repeatedly. At some point, it becomes annoying to your ears. That's what complaining sounds like: a nonstop, bothersome tune. It's okay to vent occasionally because it helps you express yourself and provides temporary relief, but habitually complaining creates a damaging emotional and physical environment. It forces you to focus on problems rather than seek solutions, and it can also lead to mental strain. When you constantly complain, your brain is being rewired to reproduce negativity, which can affect your contentment.

Not only does complaining affect you, but it also affects your relationships. It can be emotionally taxing for others to listen to your problems without any constructive action. The energy required to constantly hear your complaints can be overwhelming and may lead to emotional distance. Be mindful of how your complaining affects others. In some cases, it can be contagious and spread to those around you, creating an unpleasant atmosphere. Stop dwelling on your problems and focus on finding solutions. Choosing not to complain helps you take control of your mindset and encourages you to address issues in a healthy way.

Ways to refrain from complaining:

1. Acknowledge the problem, but don't dwell on it. Give yourself a few minutes to feel frustrated, then shift your focus to action.

2. Identify solutions—ask yourself, "What can I do to solve this issue that I have?"

3. Practice gratitude even during moments of adversity. Identify three things going right while dealing with what's going wrong.

4. Reframe your thinking—look at problems as an opportunity to learn and grow.

Stop Complaining

What do I find myself complaining about most often?

Is this something that is within my control?

If so, what can I do about this problem?

If not, am I willing to let it go to focus on my peace?

Everything is Not an Attack

It may feel or seem like it, but everything is not an attack. For example, when a friend mentions that you seem stressed, they could be offering support, not judgment. You might struggle with feeling that people are attacking you because you constantly feel criticized or judged. Have you ever stopped to think that maybe these individuals genuinely love and care about you, and that's why they're speaking up? Not every criticism or disagreement is meant to harm you. It is important to recognize when individuals are sincerely expressing their thoughts, setting boundaries, or providing constructive feedback.

Feeling attacked can cause you to respond with defensiveness, which can damage relationships and hinder personal growth. It can also cause you to react emotionally rather than logically, which can lead to poor choices like unnecessarily ending relationships or avoiding situations that require accountability. Being open to feedback, even when it is uncomfortable, helps you to evolve. When you stop assuming that everything is an attack against you, you gain peace, confidence, and better relationships.

Struggling with feeling attacked:

1. Pause before reacting and assess the situation.
2. Consider the intent: ask yourself, "Is this meant to be offensive?" or simply ask the individual about their intent.

3. Learn to accept constructive criticism by asking yourself: "What can I learn from this? And how might this help me grow?"

4. Acknowledge that even poorly delivered feedback might contain truth worth considering.

Everything is Not an Attack

Am I reflecting before I react?

What situations or feedback do I tend to take personally, even when it may not be meant that way?

Are my emotional responses based on the present moment, or are they influenced by past hurt?

What They Think of You

If you allowed your emotions to shift every time someone had a negative or wrong opinion about you, you would be on an emotional roller coaster. Why would you allow people who barely have a sense of themselves to impact how you feel about yourself? Your worth or value does not derive from someone else's perspective. People's opinions and thoughts about you will fluctuate depending on the circumstances. There are billions of people on this earth, and unfortunately, you will not be able to please them all. When you try to please everyone, you begin to diminish your authenticity because you find yourself changing who you are to accommodate others.

Let them think, feel, and believe whatever they desire about you, as long as you know your truth. People will often criticize you as a reflection of their fears, insecurities, or limitations.

Their judgments about you will never surpass what you believe about yourself, because you know who you are and what's true about you. This mindset shift takes practice; you won't master it overnight. But each time you choose your own truth over someone else's opinion, you strengthen your emotional independence.

How to drown out negative judgments:

1. Know who you are—what are your values? What do you stand for? Be confident in yourself.

2. Ignore it consciously—don't internalize every criticism, most people's opinions are based on limited information or projection.

3. Protect your energy—be intentional about who and what you allow in your emotional space.

4. Reaffirm your truth by reminding yourself of your core qualities and talking to people who truly know your character.

What They Think of you?

Their opinions may be loud, but my truth is louder:

How much of my identity has been shaped by the opinions or expectations of others?

Am I living for approval or alignment?

When People Show You Who They Are, Believe Them

The biggest mistake people make in life is focusing on a person's potential instead of their reality. Potential is hypothetical, meaning it's not real, and it can lead to a lot of disappointment. It's vital to pay attention to a person's actions, patterns, and behaviors. This means trusting what you see and the experiences you've encountered.

If you constantly see someone being dishonest with others, what makes you believe they wouldn't be dishonest with you? Don't repeatedly give someone the benefit of the doubt when they've shown you a consistent pattern. Having high expectations for someone who consistently shows you they are undeserving is self-inflicted disillusionment.

When you make excuses for a person's behavior or fail to recognize the negative patterns, you are enabling and reinforcing the behavior. This not only hinders them but also emotionally affects you. Believe the reality of the situation, not the hope or assumption of it. This doesn't mean you should become cynical or suspicious of everyone. It means being realistic about who people are based on their consistent actions. This mindset ultimately protects your emotional well-being and allows you to invest your energy in people who deserve it.

How to apply this principle:

1. Let go of your illusions about who you want them to be.

2. Pay attention to actions, not just words.

3. Don't try to fix or change people.

4. Manage your expectations.

When People Show You Who They Are, Believe Them

Think of a time when someone showed you their true character through actions, words, or repeated behavior, but you chose to ignore or excuse it.

What did you see? What did you tell yourself instead?

What were the signs or red flags you overlooked?

PART 2

The Breaking

Healing & Letting Go

It's Okay to Not Be Okay

---•-●-●•-•---

The expression "it's okay to not be okay" means that it is normal and acceptable to feel certain emotions, such as sadness, anxiety, shame, and other undesirable feelings. You must acknowledge that being human comes with ups and downs. As you continue to live life, you will recognize that every day is not going to be a good day. Life has its challenges that will leave you doubting yourself and your abilities. However, when you are struggling with those challenging periods of your life, know that it's okay if you are not okay.

Give yourself permission to feel those emotions, and if they become unbearable, seek help. While it's normal to have difficult periods, if you're consistently struggling or having thoughts of self-harm, please reach out to a mental health professional.

What is not okay is suppressing and ignoring your feelings because you don't want to seem vulnerable or weak.

Acknowledging and being honest about your emotions is the first step toward healing and growth. When you are not okay, take the time to sit with your feelings, learn from the situation, and use the experience to build resilience for the future.

Tips for being okay with not being okay:

1. Self-acceptance: Accept that struggles, setbacks, and difficult emotions are normal parts of the human experience.

2. Remind yourself that the pain is temporary.

3. Seek help: Reach out to trusted friends, family, or professionals who can provide support and validate your experiences.

It's Okay to Not Be Okay

Take a moment and ask yourself:

What am I feeling right now without judgment?

Am I okay?

What have I been trying to suppress, hide, or push through instead of allowing myself to feel?

Healing is Not Linear

Your healing is a process, and if it's done restoratively, it may take time. Whether you're healing from the loss of a loved one, a pet, or a failed relationship, you must give yourself grace. There's no straightforward path to healing. Healing looks different for everyone. There's also no specific format or time limit one must follow for their healing journey to evolve. In most cases, healing is a lifetime process because an individual may never get over losing someone or something they love, but they simply must manage living without them. Healing is not about forgetting or erasing your past; it's about finding a way to live beyond it.

The process of healing can be uncomfortable as you unpack trauma, revisit pain, and let go of false beliefs about yourself. However, be honest with yourself so you can begin to release the suffering. Don't allow others to negatively influence how you decide to heal or tell you how long your healing process should take. The amount of time it takes you, or the path you choose to heal, is for you to decide.

Healing encompasses breakthroughs, ups and downs, and setbacks. One day, you may feel like you're completely fine, whole, and happy. And the next day, you may feel like you're struggling, broken, and uneasy. The smallest things can trigger someone who is healing and cause a setback. That's normal, and it's okay. The most important thing is that you are taking care of your emotions and using your healthy coping tools to help you move forward.

Things to remember about healing:

1. Healing is not linear, and it's not a race.

2. Some days you may feel strong, and some days you may be fragile. They are both a part of the process.

3. For some, healing happens through connection with loved ones, and for others, it's found in solitude and reflection. Both approaches are valid.

4. Give yourself grace, compassion, and time.

Healing is not linear

Am I giving myself the time, the space, and the opportunity to heal?

What does healing look like for me versus what others say it should look like?

Where am I in my healing process?

What new perspective can I incorporate into my healing journey?

Let It Go

———— •◦●◦• ————

Whatever it is or whoever it is, I encourage you to let it go. That person who wronged you no longer deserves to take up space in your mind. That situation has happened, and there's nothing more you can do about it. Don't allow it to steal another moment of your joy and mental peace. When you hold on to people or situations that are not serving you, you are holding on to resentment, bitterness, unforgiveness, anger, regret, and countless other toxic emotions. The distress caused by not letting go prevents you from healing and living your best life. It creates a cycle of emotional pain, leading to more intense feelings that are fueled by avoidance.

Breaking free starts with recognizing what's holding you captive. Figure out why you are holding on to it. Acknowledge your feelings because they are valid. Then understand that you have a choice to let it go, heal, and move forward with your life without bringing baggage with you.

Letting go requires a great deal of self-awareness, as sometimes your thoughts and emotions are involuntary and unintentional. You must offer yourself consistent reassurance and use healthy coping skills. That situation, person, or experience can no longer claim your attention, peace, or happiness.

Tips for letting go:

1. Recognize what you are struggling to let go of.

2. Identify and acknowledge your emotions, thoughts, and feelings towards the situation.

3. Accept the situation for what it is; this doesn't mean you agree with it, but you are choosing to take the necessary steps to heal from it because you know you can't change the situation.

4. Make a conscious decision to use healthy strategies that help you release the negative energy of holding on. This might include journaling your feelings, seeking therapy, practicing meditation, or creating new daily routines that don't revolve around the pain.

Let It Go

Take time to reflect on what's holding you back:

What am I still holding on to that no longer serves me (pain, people, regrets, or expectations)?

How has holding on to this affected my growth, peace, or relationships?

Give Yourself Grace

———••◦●◦••———

Grace is the act of being understanding, compassionate, and patient with yourself. It's treating yourself with the same kindness you'd offer a precious friend in crisis. It means recognizing that you are human and capable of making mistakes. It's knowing you will not always get it right and will sometimes fall, stumble, and question yourself. Grace means forgiving yourself even when you feel like you don't deserve it. It's about choosing kindness over self-criticism. It's also about progress, not perfection. Grace is when you don't allow your flaws to define you, but you embrace your challenges to learn and grow from them. Grace is understanding that you don't have to have it all together. It's allowing yourself to move at your own pace. Grace is giving yourself the patience and gentleness that comes with growth. It's releasing yourself from emotional baggage and the hurts of your past. Grace makes room for you to heal, breathe, and move forward without shame.

Give yourself grace when you need a break, when you need to rest, when you've made a mistake, when you're not feeling well, or when you're unsure of your purpose or direction. Give yourself grace when you've missed a deadline or forgotten something. Give yourself grace when you can't emotionally, physically, or financially show up for yourself or others the way you want to—especially when you have nothing left to give. Give yourself grace when you're struggling.

If you have nothing else to offer in the moment, always remember to give yourself grace. You are human, and you are a work in progress.

How to give yourself grace:

1. Be gentle with yourself—talk to yourself like you would someone you love.

2. Release unrealistic expectations and acknowledge that you are consistently doing your best.

3. Rest, but don't wait until you're exhausted—use it to recharge and not recover from depletion. Preventive rest is self-care; reactive rest is damage control.

4. Practice self-forgiveness daily—when you catch yourself in self-criticism, pause and consciously choose a gentler response.

Give Yourself Grace

Grace over guilt:

What does it look like for me to give myself grace in this season?

Why do I tend to be hard on myself but compassionate to others in the same situation?

What expectations am I placing on myself that may be unfair or unrealistic?

Forgiveness Does Not Mean Reconciliation

Forgiveness is about letting go of hurt, resentment, or the desire for revenge so it no longer controls your emotions. Forgiveness is a gift you give yourself, not them. It does not require the other person to apologize or acknowledge their wrongdoing. Often, we struggle with forgiveness because we feel we are owed an apology or some form of recognition for our hurt. Most people call it "closure." However, some people will never acknowledge their poor actions, so waiting for an apology will keep you stuck and take away time from your healing.

Reconciliation is about both parties agreeing to settle their differences. In some cases, reconciliation may not be safe, suitable, or healthy if a person is unwilling to change or has done a great deal of damage. Forgiveness does not mean you have to let someone back into your life or justify their bad behaviors. It is about healing, not excusing. Forgiveness is about accepting what has happened, learning from it, and moving forward in peace. You can forgive someone to free yourself from emotional pain, but you don't have to reconcile if it is not safe or in your best interest.

Best practices for forgiveness

1. Recognize your feelings—identify what happened, how it made you feel, and why it hurt.

2. Release the need for an apology—their acknowledgement is not required for your healing.

3. Learn from the situation and set boundaries—both with yourself (what you'll accept) and others (what access they have to you.)

4. Understand that healing takes time—Forgiveness is not a one-time act, but a continuous act depending on the hurt.

Remember: You can forgive someone and still choose to protect yourself from them. Forgiveness and boundaries can coexist.

Forgiveness Does Not Mean Reconciliation

Think about this and answer honestly:

Is there someone I need to forgive—not for their sake, but for mine?

With whom have I confused forgiveness with repeated harm?

Accept People for Who They Are or Leave Them Where They're At

———•◆◆•———

When someone's values, lifestyle, or behavior do not align with yours, you have two choices: accept them for who they are, or walk away and leave them where they are. Trying to force someone to change to be who you want them to be only causes frustration, resentment, and toxicity. Staying in someone's life and expecting them to be someone they're not, just to meet your expectations, is not fair to them.

It's okay to inspire someone, but you can't force growth or improvement upon them. Change happens when someone is willing and ready, not when they are pressured. Sometimes, we must acknowledge and accept that everyone has flaws and that no one is perfect. It is up to you to determine which flaws are dealbreakers for you and then act accordingly. Deciding whether to accept someone for who they are or to walk away from the relationship is about you and what is best for your mental and emotional health. The decision is not about them; it is about your peace and what you are willing to accept in your life.

Things to know about accepting others or leaving them:

1. Practice self-awareness—understand what your expectations and desires are.

2. Everyone has imperfections, so identify what your dealbreakers are.

3. Communicate your boundaries and feelings clearly. You can accept people's flaws without accepting their mistreatment of you.

4. Prioritize your well-being and make decisions based on what serves your growth, not what feels familiar or comfortable.

Accept People for Who They Are or Leave Them Where They're At

Is there someone in my life whom I am hoping will change?

What expectations do I have of them that they consistently don't meet?

How has this affected me emotionally?

Takers Don't Have Limits

Takers are individuals who don't believe in limits. More importantly, they don't respect yours. They have minimal regard for others or their boundaries. They will take your time, energy, money, and anything else you have that benefits them. They've mastered the art of making their needs feel like your emergencies. They find ways to talk about their problems so you can offer whatever it is they need. They drain you with their issues until you agree to help them again and again. They promise to pay you back but rarely do. They often feel entitled, believing that because of their connection to you, you are obligated to help them.

Most of the time, these takers never stop needing something or experiencing issues. It's because they don't take the time to identify the root cause of their problems or work to prevent them from happening. Their only focus is on making someone else feel guilty for their situation. The thing is, at some point, you must be able to say enough is enough and recognize when you are being taken advantage of. Stop offering, stop listening, and stop enabling. You can still be a giver, but have limits. It is your responsibility to make sure you are connecting with individuals who are genuine and reciprocal. Your kindness should never be mistaken for weakness, and your generosity should never become their entitlement.

How to deal with takers:

1. Recognize the patterns—Pay attention to how you feel after interactions. Consistent feelings of being drained, resentful, or used are red flags that shouldn't be ignored.

2. Takers don't have limits, so you must define yours and be firm about them.

3. Be consistent with your boundaries—saying no to them is saying yes to yourself. You're not responsible for managing their crisis or emotions.

4. Limit your accessibility, protect your peace by limiting how much of yourself you give out.

Takers Don't Have Limits

Where do I draw the line for my peace, favors, and energy?

Who in my life constantly takes more than they give? How do I feel about this relationship?

After spending time with this person, do I feel energized or depleted?

In what ways have I sacrificed my own needs to avoid confrontation or to keep the peace?

Watch the Company You Keep

The people you associate with say a lot about who you are. Whether you recognize it or not, habits, attitudes, and behaviors are transferable and influence your life. You reflect the people you surround yourself with. Bad company can cause corruption and lead you to lose everything you've worked hard for, while good company tends to empower you and generate a positive force. If you want to prosper and elevate in your life, examine the company you are keeping.

Ask yourself: Are the individuals you surround yourself with living lives that inspire and motivate you to be better? Do these individuals encourage you to reach your dreams and aspirations? If not, it may be time to find a new circle of people who are aligned with your mission and vision for your life. A simple fact of life is that some people cannot go where you are going, and some don't want to go because they're content with their life. Don't be afraid to leave people behind. They will be right where you left them if you ever need to go back. Remember, it's better to be alone than in the wrong company.

How to choose your circle wisely:

1. Evaluate current relationships honestly—identify which relationships drain your energy or encourage negative behaviors, then create distance or remove yourself entirely.

2. Seek like-minded individuals who share your values and goals—look for people who challenge you to grow, not just people who are comfortable.

3. Lead by example and become the person you want to attract—your character and behavior will naturally draw people who match your energy and vision.

4. Be intentional about your time—invest more energy into relationships that inspire growth and less in those that keep you stagnant.

Watch the Company You Keep

Am I connecting with people who are in alignment with my purpose?

Do I surround myself with people who challenge me to be better or people who keep me stuck in old habits?

Has there ever been a time that I made a decision based on someone else's influence that I later regretted? What did I learn from this situation?

PART 3

The Shift

Mindset & Mental Habits

Stop Worrying

W orrying is a mental habit that involves a cycle of repetitive, fear-based thoughts. It's your mind's way of trying to solve problems that don't exist yet. Most people worry about future outcomes related to situations that may never happen, while others spend a lot of time worrying about things that are out of their control. Overthinking is a form of worrying that keeps you in a mental spiral, constantly replaying the would've, could've, and should've.

When you learn to trust in yourself and stop trying to control everything, it decreases your worry. The constant pressure to do more, be better, and fix things causes extreme stress. Worry is a thief. It steals your joy, your time, and your focus, leaving you mentally drained and emotionally exhausted. Worrying does not take away tomorrow's problems, but it robs you of today's presence. Give yourself grace so you can release the anxiety of perfection and protect your peace. Relaxing is a part of taking care of your body, your mind, and your emotions. Feed your faith, not your fears.

Struggling with worry:

1. Release your worries by dumping them on paper or by creating a worry window—designate 10 minutes daily to acknowledge your worries, then close your window and redirect your energy.

2. Ask yourself: Can I do something about this right now? If yes, take action. If no, practice letting it go.

3. Disrupt your worry with movement—walk, dance, or stretch.

4. Create a calm down toolkit—look at relaxing pictures, speak affirmations, listen to a soothing playlist.

Stop Worrying

Are my thoughts keeping me stuck?

What do I tend to worry about the most? Are these things within my control?

What has worrying cost me? (Time, sleep, peace)

What can I do to start trusting my process even if I don't have all the answers?

An Idle Mind

An idle mind refers to wandering, unoccupied, and unstructured thoughts with no purpose, which causes your mind to drift into worry, negativity, and self-doubt. An idle mind is a breeding ground for holistic destruction in your life. Your mind can stimulate every part of your body internally and externally. Allowing your mind to reproduce unhealthy thought patterns can ultimately affect you psychologically, emotionally, and physically. It causes you to be more susceptible to temptation and negative influences.

An idle mind is vulnerable and can manifest as procrastination, decision paralysis, or getting stuck in cycles of rumination that prevent forward progress. It will convince you that you're not good enough, that you're stuck, or that you don't deserve the good things. Having a busy mind doesn't mean it's purposeful.

Take control of your mind and be intentional about your thoughts. Your mind is one of the most powerful tools you have as a human. Create a positive and engaging mindset by feeding your mind with clarity, purpose, and direction. Know that you can train your mind to be purposeful rather than idle. When you direct your mental energy intentionally, you transform your mind from a source of chaos into a tool for growth.

Here are four essential practices to cultivate an engaged, purposeful mind:

1. Practice daily affirmations and consciously redirect negative thoughts to positive ones.

2. Embrace curiosity and learn something new.

3. Set daily goals so you have something to focus on.

4. Practice mindfulness or meditation to train your awareness and redirect wandering thoughts toward the present moment.

An Idle Mind

What am I thinking about?

Am I able to recognize when my mind is idle? What are the warning signs or triggers that indicate my mind is starting to wander into unproductive territory?

What patterns do I notice in my idle thoughts? Do they gravitate toward worry, self-doubt, or negativity?

How can I redirect my mind when I notice that it is idle?

Practice Positive Affirmations

••●●••

Positive affirmations are short statements that make you feel better about yourself. Consistently using affirmations trains your brain to focus on optimism and helps boost your self-confidence. Repeating positive affirmations helps challenge and replace negative thinking. They help you believe in yourself by serving as a reminder of your strengths and capabilities. Don't underestimate the power of reinforcement.

Let your affirmations be a part of your daily routine. Choose three to five affirmations that resonate with you personally, and repeat them each morning or during moments when negative thoughts arise. The key is consistency, not quantity. If you struggle with negative self-talk, low self-esteem, or mental health challenges, practicing positive affirmations may have a powerful impact that cultivates a resilient mindset.

Here are some examples of powerful affirmations that you can adopt or use as inspiration to create your own:

1. I am enough just like I am.

2. I trust that challenges lead to growth and better opportunities.

3. I am grateful for all that is good in my life.

4. I take steps every day towards my goals.

5. I am not who they say I am, I am who I say I am.

Practice Positive Affirmations

The intentional truths you choose to believe about yourself:

Are your core beliefs about yourself positive or negative? What specific negative beliefs do you need to challenge and replace?

Write three of your own affirmations that you can repeat to yourself. When during your day will you practice these affirmations?

After consistently practicing these affirmations for 30 days, how do you want to feel?

Know Your Worth

Knowing your worth is about understanding your value so you never settle for less. It means accepting all the components that make you who you are, regardless of your flaws or external opinions. When you know your worth, it builds confidence and empowers you to connect with people who support your values. Your worth is not determined by how others define you. It is your responsibility to identify the values and principles that set the foundation for who you are and what you believe in. Furthermore, you must recognize that everything about you is valuable, including your time, energy, and presence. One of the most important ways to honor your worth is through the boundaries you establish.

Setting boundaries is an aspect of knowing your worth because you are teaching others how to treat you. That is how you set limits on what you will and will not accept. Demand your respect by refusing to tolerate disrespect, manipulation, or involvement in situations that diminish your self-confidence. Do not cling to things or people that are not serving you. Be willing to walk away from anyone or anything that does not align with your worth if necessary. Do not settle for less than you deserve to accommodate others. Your worth is inherent and unchangeable. It is not something you earn or lose based on external circumstances.

Connecting with your worth:

1. Set standards for your life and be firm about them—in relationships, career, and personal goals.

2. Validate yourself and don't let others define you—practice self-compassion and acknowledge your achievements.

3. Disconnect from anything that makes you question your worth or doesn't align with it—this includes toxic relationships, negative environments, and limiting situations.

4. Regularly remind yourself of your accomplishments, strengths, and the positive impact you have on others.

Know Your Worth

Am I honoring my worth?

What makes me valuable? What unique strengths, qualities, and contributions do I bring to the world?

Have I accepted anything in the past that was beneath my values? What caused me to settle?

What specific changes will I start making today that will align with my worth?

Be Your Own Muse

Imagine becoming the example you are searching for: someone bold, creative, and rich in spirit. Don't wait for someone to inspire you when you are the inspiration. Are you sitting around waiting for someone else to give you your praises, when you should be giving them to yourself? Being your own muse means showing up for yourself, encouraging yourself, and believing in yourself.

It's about loving, appreciating, and accepting all that comes with you, both the good and the bad. It means recognizing your power, your capabilities, and your worth, while being proud of yourself regardless of your outcomes. Imagine wanting a hand clap from someone who has no intention of clapping for you. Some people will refuse to acknowledge your significance, no matter how great you are. This is why it is important to be your own muse so you don't rely on external validation, which can lead to disappointment.

The same energy, attention, and engagement that you give others for their growth should be given to yourself as well. It's okay to support and admire others, but make sure you are feeding your soul too. You are a masterpiece that is priceless and precious. So, live your life knowing how amazing you are, whether others acknowledge it or not.

How to be your own muse:

1. Take care of yourself—understand who you are, learn to support yourself, and be kind to yourself.

2. Those qualities you admire in others, start embodying them. Be the energy you are drawn to. It's not about comparing or copying, but more about creating.

3. Celebrate your wins (big and small)—Take time to acknowledge your progress, no matter how small.

4. Acknowledge and accept your faults while learning from them. This is what helps you grow and become more confident.

Be Your Own Muse

Am I lighting my own fire?

If I were someone else's inspiration, what would I want them to take away from me?

How can I celebrate and encourage myself the way I would someone else I deeply admire?

What can I do to start living more boldly and unapologetically?

Focus on the Present

Stop worrying about the past or the future. The past is gone, and the future is yet to come. Understand that you cannot change the past, nor can you control the future. Don't miss the excitement of the present moment by dwelling on the past or contemplating the future. The only moment you truly have power over is right now.

There may be times when the present is not ideal, but when you learn to make the best of your circumstances, it can help distract you from overthinking. To focus on the here and now, one productive approach is to limit distractions and give the situation at hand your full attention. When we are mentally scattered, thinking about what we should have done yesterday or what might go wrong tomorrow, we lose our ability to think clearly, make intentional choices, and truly connect with ourselves and others.

Being present sharpens your focus, helps you gain mental clarity, and allows you to fully engage with what's happening now because you are not weighed down by past regrets or future anxieties. Furthermore, it helps you feel more conscious and connected to reality.

Ways to redirect your attention to the present moment:

1. Practice mindfulness, meditation, and grounding techniques that anchor you in the present moment.

2. Eliminate distractions and avoid multitasking. Give your full attention to one task at a time.

3. Accept what you cannot change, and focus on the influence you have right now.

4. Stay organized and create systems that support mental clarity. When your environment is clear, your mind can focus better.

Focus on The Present

Take a moment to ground yourself. Breathe deeply. Then reflect:

What thoughts, worries, or distractions are pulling me away from the present?

How can I gently bring myself back to the now when I notice my mind wandering?

When fully present, what do I notice about my surroundings, thoughts, or feelings?

What is Meant to Be, Will Be

Train your mind to accept this: what you're truly meant to achieve will align with your efforts, values, and timing. "What is meant to be, will be" isn't about fate deciding for you. It's about being in alignment with your authentic path and putting in consistent effort toward what genuinely serves your highest good. If something doesn't happen, it simply wasn't aligned with your path. However, to receive what's meant for you, you must believe you deserve it and be willing to work for it.

When you declare the desires of your heart to be true, you must create a plan, take action, and trust your process. Let those things flow naturally to you. Don't try to force, coerce, or manipulate the situation. Instead, trust, believe, and have faith in yourself, your abilities, and your higher being. Most importantly, you must put in consistent effort toward the things you are hoping for. Be patient, and know that when the time is right, whatever is meant to be will be.

How to embody this philosophy:

1. Dream with clarity—get specific about what you want and why.

2. Align your beliefs with your goals—address limiting beliefs that block your path.

3. Work hard and strategically toward your vision.

4. Trust in divine timing—stay patient and open to how and when things unfold.

What is Meant to Be, Will Be

Am I doing my best and letting life take care of the rest?

Do I truly believe that what's for me will come in the right way at the right time?

What situations in my life have I been trying to force or control instead of working hard and trusting my process?

What dreams or goals am I ready to pursue with dedicated effort and patient trust?

Be Intentional

——————••◆••——————

Let everything you do have purpose and direction, so it bears fruit in your life. This means moving through life with conscious awareness rather than reactively. Your actions, words, and thoughts should be intentional and aligned with your purpose. You have control over the things you speak, think, and the way you behave. Let these things align with your goals, values, and growth.

Being intentional means consciously thinking things through before acting on them. It means having a process, a plan, or some direction for the moves you make. When you operate with mindless and aimless behavior, you find yourself making careless and repetitive decisions, which leads to a state of autopilot. Imagine being absent from your own life, feeling dull, with no sense of fulfillment because you lack intention. It's time to start living your life on purpose.

When you move with purpose, you are able to build clarity, become more self-aware, and accomplish goals. Furthermore, it creates feelings of hopefulness and confidence. Be intentional with your life, your relationships, your energy, and everything else that makes you who you are. When you live intentionally, every day becomes a deliberate step toward the life you truly want to create.

How to be more intentional:

1. Be specific about what you want and why it matters to you.

2. Set SMART goals that support your vision and values for your life.

3. Make purposeful choices—pause to think before you speak and act, and eliminate distractions when making important decisions.

4. Practice regular self-reflection to monitor progress and adjust your approach as needed.

Be Intentional

Am I living on purpose and with purpose?

What areas of my life am I being intentional in, and what areas am I operating on autopilot?

Am I spending energy on things that don't reflect my priorities or my purpose?

PART 4

The Building

Boundaries, Habits & Growth

Learn to Say No

———— ••●•• ————

Saying no is an important skill for setting boundaries that helps protect your time, energy, and well-being. You must recognize your limits and understand your priorities. Do not overburden yourself trying to please others. Most people struggle with saying no because they want to avoid conflict, guilt, or discomfort. Usually, when individuals fail to say no, they feel taken advantage of and blame others for feeling depleted. However, the only person to blame is the one in the mirror for overextending themselves. This reflects not just our choices but also our patterns of self-neglect. Understanding why we struggle with this boundary is the first step toward change.

Many reasons exist why individuals struggle with saying no and fail to realize the harm it causes. Not saying no to avoid conflict only creates internal friction. Setting boundaries and prioritizing your own needs when necessary does not mean you are not a nice person. Saying no and being a nice person are independent of each other. You can still be courteous while saying no. When you learn to say no to things that don't serve you in the present moment, you reduce your stress while building self-respect.

If you struggle with saying no, here are some skills you can utilize to assist:

1. Evaluate what is being asked of you and ask yourself—Am I truly interested in doing this, and will this be a burden to me?

2. Offer alternatives if feasible.

Example: "I am not able to cook for you on Wednesday, but I am available on Thursday if that works for you."

3. Be polite, direct, and confident.

   Example: "Thank you for thinking of me, but unfortunately, I will not be able to make it to your event next week."

4. No is sometimes a complete sentence; you don't always need to provide explanations.

Learn to Say No

"What makes it hard for me to say no, and what would change if I felt more confident doing it?"

Think of a recent situation where you said "yes" when you really wanted to say "no." What triggered that decision?

How might things change if you started saying no more confidently and respectfully?

Know the Difference: Requirements vs Expectations

There is a major difference between what you require and what you expect. Requirements ensure that your needs are being met, while expectation is the hope that your needs will be met. Requirements are standards you hold for yourself and should be non-negotiable. Knowing your requirements means being clear about your needs in relationships, environments, and opportunities so that you feel safe, respected, and valued. Requirements are your boundaries and should always be clearly communicated. They help protect your peace and reduce disappointment. However, you must ensure that you are enforcing these requirements.

On the other hand, expectations are built on hope, assumptions, and unspoken desires. Expectations are the equivalent of wishful thinking. Unmet expectations can lead to frustration and broken relationships because a person failed to speak up about their needs. Don't allow your expectations to force you to settle. Be clear, direct, and intentional about your requirements.

Strategies to uphold your requirements vs your expectations:

1. Identify your non-negotiables and create a list of your top 5 relationship or personal requirements (e.g., honest communication, emotional support, mutual respect.)

2. Don't assume others know your needs, communicate early, and be honest.

3. Set boundaries with your requirements and stand firm on your consequences.

Know the Difference: Requirements vs Expectations

Am I clear about my requirements and releasing my expectations?

Have I ever assumed someone "should know better"? Would this be considered an unfair expectation rather than a clear requirement? Why?

What's one expectation I can let go of that's causing me unnecessary stress or disappointment?

Be Proactive and Not Reactive

———•◦•◦•———

Life will always have its trials and tribulations, but there is nothing better than being prepared for adversity. It is always best to have control over your life rather than letting your life control you. Being proactive means having the discernment to anticipate issues and plan to prevent them from happening.

Being proactive requires you to be intentional and action-focused, which helps to reduce or eliminate problems before they arise. It creates a sense of empowerment when you feel in control of the things happening to you and around you. Being proactive gives you the authority to dictate the narrative of your story. When you foresee an issue occurring, the best thing to do is to act on it so that it does not disrupt you in the future.

Reactive refers to your response after an issue has already occurred without prior planning or thought. Having a reactive mindset leaves you feeling overloaded because you wait for a crisis to happen before you act. This leads to powerless feelings because you are constantly being controlled by your circumstances. Don't wait around for a disaster to happen. Instead, take proactive steps and find ways to prevent it from happening.

How to become more proactive and less reactive:

1. Be intentional about your days—don't just roll into them. Plan ahead.

2. If you can predict it, then prepare for it.

3. Act immediately when you notice an upcoming problem; waiting too long keeps you in reactive mode.

4. Reflect regularly and use your insight to improve your proactive skills.

Be Proactive and Not Reactive

Is my life operating by preparation or pressure?

Have I ever experienced a time when being proactive saved me from a bigger problem? What encouraged me to be proactive?

Was there ever a time I waited after an issue occurred, and it caused more problems than it would have if I were proactive?

Habit Formation

Your habits are either working for you or against you. If you want to create lasting change, you must learn to form healthy habits. Habit formation uses repetition to generate automatic behaviors. Small, repeated actions done consistently help shape your future. One decision, one routine, one choice over time builds discipline, confidence, and growth. When you do something often enough, your brain wires it as your new normal.

Whether you realize it or not, every day you are building habits through the things you do. For example, brushing your teeth, making coffee in the morning, or reading a book before bed. The habit doesn't have to be massive to make a difference. Tiny actions done regularly can lead to substantial outcomes. The more you engage in your habit, the less conscious effort it requires. Your daily routine can support the development of your habit. Find a way to include it in your routine to help you stay consistent until it becomes natural.

Essentials for habit formation:

1. Start small and be specific.

2. Make your habit hard to ignore, make it obvious, and create reminders.

3. Habit stack—attach your new habit to something that you already do consistently.

4. Be persistent, but also be patient.

5. Track your progress—this builds motivation and momentum.

Habit Formation

Discipline over destruction:

What's one habit I want to form? And why?

What's a bad habit that is holding me back? What am I getting out of this bad habit?

Set SMART Goals

Setting SMART goals gives you a sense of purpose and helps build motivation. Rather than setting vague intentions that lead nowhere, SMART goals provide structure for real progress. They create a process and plan for you to accomplish your goals. The acronym SMART stands for specific, measurable, achievable, relevant, and time-bound. Setting SMART goals can be a valuable tool when aiming for success. Your goals should be **specific** so there is no ambiguity in what you are working toward. You want to make sure your goals are **measurable** to help you keep up with your progress and identify any changes that need to be made.

Make sure the goals are **achievable** and realistic so you don't set yourself up for failure. The goals need to be attainable for you. Every goal should have **relevance** and contribute to your broader purpose. This gives your goals meaning and keeps you motivated because you understand that once you achieve them, they will be impactful. Set a clear time frame for when you want to accomplish your goals. Having a deadline allows you to measure progress and stay on schedule. This decreases procrastination and encourages you to prioritize your tasks. Other helpful strategies include writing your SMART goals down and reviewing them daily to maintain focus and track progress. Turn your visions into results by setting SMART goals!

Example of a SMART goal:

Goal: I will save $200 each month for the next six months to increase my savings

Specific: I will save $200

Measurable: $200 each month

Achievable: 2 paychecks in a month, saving $100 from each paycheck, is manageable.

Relevance: Supports my broader financial security goal

Time-Bound: Six-month time frame

Set SMART Goals

Am I making my goals make sense?

What prevents me from setting SMART goals? Why?

What goal(s) have I been wanting to pursue?

What goals have I set in the past that I was not able to accomplish? What have I learned from this?

Have Confidence in Your Decisions

———•◦•———

Have you ever decided to do something, confided in someone about your plans, and they talked you out of it or made you second-guess yourself? Prematurely discussing your decisions can cause you to question or doubt them, especially if you're speaking with someone who doesn't understand the vision. Sometimes the plans you choose for yourself are only understood by you. You have more information and guidance about your life than others, so there will be times when they "don't get it," and that's okay—because it may not be meant for them to get it.

In some cases, people will attempt to talk you out of your plans or tell you what they would do if they were in your situation. Imagine letting someone talk you out of your dreams, only to watch someone else with less talent, experience, and enthusiasm thrive doing the very thing you envisioned. It's better to try and fail than to never try at all. Being confident in your decisions helps you stand firm in what you believe and encourages you to resist external opposition.

Building confidence in your decisions:

1. Have a purpose for your decision—what is your why?

2. Silence others' opinions—just because someone has an opinion doesn't mean it's relevant to your situation.

3. Engage in making choices without seeking validation or others' opinions.

4. Not every decision will be perfect, but learn from each one without dwelling in regret.

Have Confidence in Your Decisions

Am I trusting my inner wisdom or struggling with self-doubt?

What holds me back from feeling confident in my choices? (ex. Fear, judgment, and perfectionism)

Is there someone else's opinion I am prioritizing over my own, and why?

When was a time I trusted my gut, and it led me in the right direction? What did I learn?

Protect Your Energy

Energy is transferable, and that's why it's important to protect yours. Your energy is your safe place and is sacred. It should fuel tranquility, happiness, and love. Always aim to multiply good energy and subtract anything that threatens it. When it comes to energy, opposites do not attract. If you have positive energy and surround yourself with someone who has consistently negative energy, they will likely drain you, whether it's intentional or not. On the other hand, someone who has a positive vibe will only add to yours. These individuals will uplift you, inspire you, and bring balance.

Protecting your peace does not include matching negative energy with negative energy. Someone else's energy reflects them, not you. Don't allow others to control your energy by mirroring their poor behaviors. When you don't protect your energy, you become consumed and drained by toxic people, unhealthy habits, and pointless disputes. Stand firm in your character by removing, eliminating, or creating distance from energy that does not align with yours. Everyone has difficult days, so be mindful of how your energy affects others, especially when you're struggling.

Steps for protecting your energy:

1. Be intentional about who and what you give your time to.

2. Remove yourself from people, places, or situations that drain your energy.

3. Fuel your positive energy by engaging with people, places, and things that bring you joy and a sense of purpose.

4. Set boundaries with yourself and others: This includes saying "no" to anything that drains you.

Protect Your Energy

Am I being selective with my access?

Do I feel guilty for protecting my energy? If so, how can I release that guilt?

When have I noticed my energy affecting others negatively, and how can I be more mindful of this?

What practices or rituals help me reconnect to myself and refill my emotional tank?

Take Care of Yourself

———••◦●◦••———

It is imperative to understand that you are the most important person in your life. Therefore, take care of you first. There are times when we drain ourselves because we want to be everything to everyone else while neglecting ourselves. You may have heard the expression "you can't pour from an empty cup," and that is true. If you neglect yourself and continue to pour into others by giving your time, attention, and energy, you will soon become empty and run down with nothing left to give.

Take time each day to give to yourself emotionally, physically, and mentally. Prioritize your needs, even if that means not being available to others. Taking care of yourself looks different for each person. Figure out what helps you feel motivated, excited, and energized, and give it to yourself daily. These things may change from season to season, so stay aware and adjust as needed. Fill yourself up and keep your cup full.

Ideas for taking care of yourself

Emotionally:

1. Practice self-compassion.

2. Recite positive affirmations.

3. Practice gratitude.

Mentally:

1. Get adequate sleep.

2. Practice mindfulness/attend therapy if possible.

3. Take breaks from social media, addictions, television, etc.

Physically:

1. Engage in physical activities (exercising, dancing, gardening.)

2. Avoid harmful products.

3. Eat a well-balanced diet and stay hydrated.

Take Care of Yourself

Take a quiet moment and reflect with honesty and compassion:

How have I been showing up for others more than I've been showing up for myself?

What does taking care of myself mean to me, not just physically, but emotionally and mentally?

What are the signs that I'm neglecting my own needs?

PART 5

The Becoming

Confidence, Elevation & Empowerment

Choose Happiness

Choosing happiness means being intentional and conscious about focusing on the positive aspects of your life. Choosing happiness isn't always easy, especially during difficult seasons, but it's about making small, purposeful shifts in how we approach our daily experiences. This includes actively engaging in strategies that promote healthy mental and emotional well-being. When you begin to choose happiness, it transforms the way you experience the world and its situations. While life will always have its challenges, choosing happiness changes the way you react to what happens to you.

A positive mindset causes you to be slow to anger and helps you tackle challenging situations with ease. It helps build better relationships by fostering joy and kindness, which makes you more sociable. While external factors can influence us, we often have more power over our emotional responses than we realize. Your happiness is a choice, so be intentional and choose it purposefully every day. Choosing happiness, in turn, means choosing love, laughter, and peace.

Practical strategies for choosing happiness include:

1. Limiting your access to negative influences—toxic people, draining environments, social media.

2. Letting go of what you can't control—focus on your responses, not others' actions.

3. Engaging in activities that bring excitement and joy—hobbies, nature, meaningful connections.

4. Practicing gratitude daily—acknowledging what's going well, even in small moments.

Choose Happiness

What does happiness truly mean to you, not what others expect it to look like, but what it feels like in your own heart?

When was the last time you genuinely felt happy? What were you doing in that moment, and who were you doing it with?

What are 3 things that bring you genuine happiness? Write them down, then schedule time for at least one of them this week.

Small Things to a Giant

When you view yourself as a giant and your problems as small things, you shift the power dynamic in your favor. Though challenges can feel overwhelming, you have more strength and resources than your problems appear to have. The reason you become overwhelmed when you're faced with adversity is that you think your problems are more powerful than you. Your problems are temporary, manageable, and powerless. The weight they carry is insignificant compared to the strength you possess to overcome them.

Recognize the control you have in any situation. Now and then, life will find a way to challenge you, whether it's a delay, a detour, or a disappointment. Do not be discouraged. Your problems are not as insurmountable as they seem. You are filled with resilience. You've survived storms that you once thought would drown you. As a giant in your own life, any issue you face in the past, present, or future can be conquered. Every problem you face is beneath your strength. No problem is bigger than you.

Conquering your problems as a giant:

1. Shift your perspective by viewing your problems as opportunities to grow rather than punishments.

2. Shrink your problems by breaking them down into smaller/manageable parts.

3. Respond to your problems thoughtfully rather than reacting emotionally.

4. Replace worrying and fear with a focus on actionable solutions.

Small Things to a Giant

My problems may seem big, but I am bigger:

What challenge felt overwhelming and unbearable in the moment, but now feels small in hindsight?

What "small things" do I need to stop giving giant energy to (rumors, drama, fear, rejection)?

What strengths make me a giant?

Celebrate People That Celebrate You

This is about reciprocation, giving and receiving mutual support. One of the best things you can do in life is to prioritize and appreciate the people who love and support you. Stop spending precious time chasing people who are indifferent or inconsistent toward you. Don't waste your time worrying about those who show you how little you mean to them. Instead, focus your energy on individuals who value and appreciate you.

Relationships should be a two-way street. This means the energy and effort must be mutual. If you have someone who consistently celebrates your wins, shows up for you in your time of need, and adds value to your life, they deserve the same in return. Make time to pour into those relationships where love, respect, and encouragement flow in both directions. Celebrate the people who recognize your worth and remind you of it.

Practice building reciprocal relationships:

1. Notice the people who root for you.

2. Reciprocate the support, love, and recognition.

3. Show thoughtfulness in small but meaningful ways—listen actively, share helpful resources, give your time.

4. Reduce energy spent on one-sided relationships.

Celebrate the People That Celebrate You

Who consistently shows up for me and celebrates my growth?

Am I reciprocating the love, energy, and support I receive?

Am I chasing validation from people who don't value me?

Elevation Requires Separation

The phrase "elevation requires separation" typically suggests that as you advance in life, you may have to part ways with some relationships, mindsets, and bad habits. This can feel difficult, but what's more difficult is remaining stuck because you continue to connect with things that no longer serve your growth and purpose. Often, the very things you struggle to release are what keep you from moving forward.

People who don't support you, bring negativity to your life, or undermine your confidence should not have access to your progress. Sometimes the separation needed isn't from others, but from your own limiting thought patterns, negative self-talk, or destructive habits. It's best to release those limiting beliefs and adopt new perspectives that foster hope and elevation. Practice releasing unhealthy routines and behaviors that interrupt your growth, and replace them with actions that support your goals. When you desire to live a prosperous life, there will be things or people you must surrender as you move forward on your journey.

How to navigate elevation through separation:

1. Identify what you need to separate from—toxic relationships, limiting beliefs, or self-sabotaging habits.

2. Create healthy distance by setting boundaries, changing routines, or limiting exposure.

3. Recognize that letting go creates space for opportunities, growth, and aligned connections.

4. Intentionally build new habits and seek relationships that support your elevated mindset.

Elevation Requires Separation

What does "elevation" look like for me right now in mindset, relationships, or goals?

What must I separate from to become who I'm meant to be?

Am I willing to feel discomfort now for the sake of becoming better later?

It's Not Too Late

As long as you have breath in your body, it's not too late to do what you have been dreaming of doing. Don't let your age, past experiences, or concerns about timing convince you that your moment has passed. These are just excuses that will hold you back from fulfilling your desires. You are exactly where you need to be. Start where you are and use what you have.

Society will have you believe that there's a timeline for everything, including buying a home, graduating from college, and having children. I love to be the bearer of good news because that timeline is fictional, unreal, and imaginative. Life does not follow a perfect schedule. In fact, most successful people have encountered bumps, hiccups, and detours along their journey. You are not behind. You are right on time. You can start over at 30, heal at 50, and even change careers at 60. It's not too late, and there's no deadline for becoming who you have been called to be.

Try these steps to shift your mind to "it's not too late."

1. Throw out that imaginary timeline.

2. Visualize how different your life could be if you believed it's never too late to pursue your dreams.

3. Take one step forward—apply for that job, send that email, or take the class.

4. Rewrite your narrative by replacing self-doubt with empowering affirmations—start saying, "I'm right on time."

It's Not Too Late

There's no deadline for what's mine:

What aspiration of mine have I buried because of age, time, or past mistakes?

In what ways can I give myself permission to keep going or start over again, without judgment?

What's one small step I can take this week toward something I thought was "too late" for me?

Do the Best You Can with What You Have

———————•••●●••———————

Don't be held back by your limitations. Instead, do your best with what you have. It's easy to overlook your resources when you're too focused on what's missing. But sometimes, you can accomplish a lot with just a little. Rather than dwelling on what you lack, shift your focus to what's available right now, such as your resources, opportunities, and hidden talents you haven't explored yet.

Focusing on what you don't have only fuels fear, leaving you paralyzed and unable to take action with your existing capabilities. Don't sit around waiting for the perfect circumstances. Instead, create the right conditions with what you currently have. People often abandon their goals, dreams, and aspirations because they believe they are not in the right position or don't have enough means. Start where you are and use what you have.

How to make the most of what you have:

1. Change your mindset from "I don't have enough" to "What can I do with what I have right now?"

2. Take inventory of your current assets—skills, connections, tools, knowledge, and even time.

3. Maximize what you have—use free online courses, leverage social media, or start small with minimal investment.

4. Stop waiting for the perfect moment and take one concrete action today.

Do the Best You Can with What You Have

Am I showing up fully, even when my circumstances are not ideal?

Where in my life am I waiting for the "perfect" moment, instead of starting with what I have?

Has there been a time in my life when I did something meaningful with limited support, energy, or time?

Embrace Change

Change is constant, inevitable, and sometimes feels overwhelming, but it's continuously happening whether you're ready or not. While some changes are genuinely difficult and require time to process, embracing change can turn many challenges into opportunities for growth. To accept the transition, you must shift your perspective to see it as an invitation to evolve, not a disruption to your life.

Resisting change can lead to stagnation and prevent you from becoming your best self. Fearing change will only keep you stuck in the same place with the same patterns and mindset that have been hindering your progress. Change can mark the end of something old and the beginning of something new. The best thing to do is embrace it, because the sooner you accept it, the easier it becomes to adapt. The key is learning to flow with it rather than fight against it. When you embrace change, you open yourself to new experiences, relationships, and opportunities that you could have never imagined.

How to successfully embrace change:

1. Stay open-minded and flexible, ask "what can this teach me?" instead of immediately resisting.

2. Focus on the potential benefits rather than fixating only on what you're losing. Recognize that change is not happening to you, it's happening for you.

3. Trust the process, recognize that change often brings gifts you couldn't have planned for yourself.

4. Take small steps, you don't have to transform overnight; gradual adaptation is still progress.

Embrace Change

How do I typically react to change?

Are there any changes in my life that I am resisting? If so, why?

Is this resistance based on fear, control, or uncertainty?

What changes have I successfully navigated in the past, and what strengths did I discover about myself?

Slow Down

Your life is not a race. It's meant to be lived, not rushed. When you're constantly chasing something, wanting quick success and instant gratification, it can cause unnecessary pressure, which leads to mental and emotional strain. Slow progress is better than no progress. Being active does not always mean you are being productive.

The quality of your work suffers when you're always in a hurry. It increases your chances of making mistakes and errors. Rushing also causes you to make poor and impulsive decisions that you may regret later. Additionally, you may feel exhausted and overwhelmed from the constant release of adrenaline.

Slowing down allows you to be more focused on the things that are important to you. It helps you make logical decisions and feel satisfied with your work. Learn to be realistic with your schedule and don't overcommit yourself. Each moment prepares you for the next. Therefore, savor the moments and remember that patience is a virtue.

Ready to slow down? Try this:

1. Stop comparing your timeline to someone else's. Your journey is unique and moves at its own pace.

2. Plan and build in buffer time.

3. Prioritize, focus on the important/urgent things first.

4. Stop overcommitting—tackle one thing at a time.

Slow Down

What beliefs have I told myself that cause me to "keep going" and prevent me from slowing down?

Are there specific times or moments that I find myself rushing throughout my day?

When was the last time I felt present and unhurried?

Afterword

---◆◆◆---

This book may be over, but your story is still being written. I want to thank you for taking the opportunity to read this book, and more importantly, for doing the work to reflect, explore, and challenge yourself. The journey does not end here. Healing, growth, and becoming your best self are lifelong processes. You will still have hard days and may be tempted to fall into old patterns, but the good thing is that now you have tools to help you stay on track. Now that you know you hold the power to create a better, healthier, and more intentional life, I encourage you to embrace that power.

Lastly, I am proud of you, and I hope you will keep going.

With love,

Dr. Sheree Johnson

www.ingramcontent.com/pod-product-compliance
Lightning Source LLC
Chambersburg PA
CBHW071325130626
46556CB00004B/1752